Restoration by Water's Edge

The Gift of Spiritual Recovery

Tony Caico

KW
KingdomWinds
PUBLISHING

Copyright © 2022 by Tony Caico

All rights reserved. No part of this publication may be reproduced, distributed, or transmitted in any form or by any means, including photocopying, recording, or other electronic or mechanical methods, without the prior written permission of the publisher, except in the case of brief quotations embodied in critical reviews and certain other noncommercial uses permitted by copyright law. For permission requests, write to the publisher at publishing@kingdomwinds.com.

Unless otherwise indicated, all Scripture references are taken from the Holy Bible, New International Version®, NIV® Copyright © 1973, 1978, 1984, 2011 by Biblica, Inc.® Used by permission. All rights reserved worldwide.

First Edition, 2022
ISBN 10: 978-1-64590-022-1
Published by Kingdom Winds Publishing.
www.kingdomwinds.com
publishing@kingdomwinds.com
Printed in the United States of America.

Special thanks for Fresh Start Ministries, the amazing place where this transformation took place.

Thanks to Pastor Joe Cordovano and his wife, Kelly Cordovano, who started this ministry where men could find a place to break their life-altering addiction through the transformative power of Jesus Christ.

To Pastor Tim Carlsward, who was my spiritual mentor for the entire year. Your kindness and toughness were exactly what I needed.

Thanks to the amazing counselors that helped me immensely through my year-long rehabilitation: Felix Vasquez, Dave Black, Enrique Aponte, Wayne Lathrop, Lucas Brown (RIP), and Leslie Hunter.

A note of gratitude for Bob Delorey, one of my brothers from the ministry. Bob's photography and collaboration added significant and sentimental value to this project.

Lastly, a special thanks to my ex-wife and her husband, Janet and Nicky Spofford. Without your love and dedication to the children, I would have never been able to take the time to reclaim my life through The Lord. I am forever grateful.

Walk with me...

Luke 5:36-39

"He told them this parable: 'No one tears a piece out of a new garment to patch an old one. Otherwise, they will have torn the new garment, and the patch from the new will not match the old. And no one pours new wine into old wineskins. Otherwise, the new wine will burst the skins; the wine will run out and the wineskins will be ruined. No, new wine must be poured into new wineskins. And no one after drinking old wine wants the new, for they say, "The old is better."'"

How long is recovery? How long is discovery? When does providence kick in? What does this mean to you?
Shedding skin, healing wounds, uncovering new paths, new life directions; trying to identify which are false and which are true.

Examining life, planning life, and living life. How much time for each?
Do we spend, should we spend in our painful and arduous search to reach?

Our true potential, and how do we really know if and when we are on the right track?
Is it a feeling? A belief? Do we tread alone or follow some pack?

We often witness others that seem to have it all figured out; they seem so pleased;
With themselves, their lives, their jobs, their faith. Surely, it's not just to appease;

The masses on the surface, while deep down inside they feel the same as you,
They've just learned to deal with life, staying positive and faithful, not taking time to stew;

Over spilt milk and past mistakes. They add new wine to new wineskins, trusting in God,
Because only He knows if we walk on green grass with roots or man-made sod;

Pretending to be someone we are not, making up new versions along the way.
When all we need to do is follow Him, NOT ourselves, just ask Him, and He will say,

"WALK WITH ME, and I will show you what I had planned for you all along."
And the more you try and do it yourself, the harder it becomes to sing your own song;

Of hope, joy, happiness, comfort, prosperity, peace—all that we seek,
But relying on our OWN way of doing things hasn't made us strong, only weak.

The secret is to LET GO and stop trying so hard. The Lord knows this task is daunting,
But the pursuit to become *who we were always meant to be* can be far less haunting;

If we trust in God, stay in His Word; it becomes much easier to follow,
Our purpose in life; He makes us whole; we are now solid inside…no longer hollow.

We've tried it OUR WAY, I know I have, and the results have left me numb,
With His help, we can sacrifice what we are now for what we *could become.*

Introduction

There are many instances in the great story of The Gospel where Jesus performed jaw-dropping miracles, but three stories specifically where He restored life and literally raised someone from the dead. That's right, He raised them from death and brought them back to life; this actually happened. If you don't believe in this principle, then the story you are about to read through a series of poems about restoration and regeneration may open your mind to what the power of God can do to change the course of a person's life. The story you are about to read is about revival, not from literal death, but certainly from spiritual death.

Let's look at the three instances where Jesus raised someone from the dead and gave them new life:

The first we find in Matthew 9:23-26:

"When Jesus entered the synagogue leader's house and saw the noisy crowd and people playing pipes, he said, 'Go away. The girl is not dead but asleep.' But they laughed at him. After the crowd had been put outside, he went in and took the girl by the hand, and she got up. News of this spread through all that region."

The second instance we find in Luke 7:11-17:

"Soon afterward, Jesus went to a town called Nain, and his disciples and a large crowd went along with him. As he approached the town gate, a dead person was being carried out—the only son of his mother, and she was a widow. And a large crowd from the town was with her. When the Lord saw her, his heart went out to her and he said, 'Don't cry.' Then he went up and touched the bier they were carrying him on, and the bearers stood still. He said, 'Young man, I say to you, get up!' The dead man sat up and began to talk, and Jesus gave him back to his mother. They were all filled with awe and praised God. 'A great prophet has appeared among us,' they said. 'God has come to help his people.' This news about Jesus spread throughout Judea and the surrounding country."

And the third miracle is the story of Lazarus: John 11:38-43:

"Jesus, once more deeply moved, came to the tomb. It was a cave with a stone laid across the entrance. 'Take away the stone,' he said. 'But, Lord,' said Martha, the sister of the dead man, 'by this time there is a bad odor, for he has been there four days.' Then Jesus said, 'Did I not tell you that if you believe, you will see the glory of God?' So they took away the stone. Then Jesus looked up and said, 'Father, I thank you that you have heard me. I knew that you always hear me, but I said this for the benefit of the people standing here, that they may believe that you sent me.' When he had said this, Jesus called in a loud voice, 'Lazarus, come out!' The dead man came out, his hands and feet wrapped with strips of linen, and a cloth around his face. Jesus said to them, 'Take off the grave clothes and let him go.'"

Clearly, raising people from the dead is not something we tend to witness these days, mainly because Jesus no longer physically walks the earth. However, that doesn't mean He's no longer in the restoration business. It doesn't mean that He is no longer reviving people. In fact, it happens every day when someone accepts Jesus into their heart as their Lord and Savior. People are resuscitated and saved daily, but for some of us, it's not until we hit rock bottom that we find ourselves ready to turn our lives over to God.

For some of us, restoration is a long and painstaking journey, one that cannot truly happen without first recovering from the painful circumstances of our past. Some of us can't handle the adversity we face, and this leads us into perpetual poor decision-making and addictive lifestyles. Before we can truly find our place with God, we need His help overcoming this pain and these addictions. Much of what is shared in this book of poetry has to do with recovery. After all, the Water's Edge referenced in the title of this book is the Christian-based rehabilitation center (Fresh Start Ministries), where I finally submitted my life to Christ and reclaimed my soul. A ministry specifically designed to help restore men recovering from addiction through the power only found in a deep and meaningful relationship with Jesus Christ. This is no small task, and what you are about to read is the story of my restoration; and how I was personally resuscitated by the Holy Spirit. It is this restoration and revival, through Jesus, that has given me the strength, perseverance, and courage to write these poems.

I pray that each reader can draw inspiration from the following pages of poems and Scriptures that have reshaped my life. I have been reborn in Christ, baptized by the Holy Spirit, and I now walk each day on the path God has laid out before me.

I hope this book touches your heart; God bless each one of you.

Ephesians 3:20-21

"Now to him who is able to do immeasurably more than all we ask or imagine, according to his power that is at work within us, to him be glory in the church and in Christ Jesus throughout all generations, for ever and ever! Amen."

Table of Contents

Walk with Me	4-5
Introdution	6-7
Warm Waters	10-11
Hourglass	12-13
Where's the FIT	14-15
Who You Have	16-17
Chasing the Rabbit	18-19
Breaking the Chains	20-21
Right Here... Right Now	22-23
Treasure Map	24-25
Rocked by Paul	26-27
Father's Day	28-29
Peace	30-31
Submerged	32-33
Back on the Bus	34-35
Face to Face by Water's Edge	36-37
Unbearable Pain No More	38-39
Codependency's Foe	40-41
The First Start "SWAT" Team	42-43
Clarity's Purpose at the Lake	44-45
Objects in the Rear-View Mirror are "Smaller" than They Appear	46-47
Grace	48-49
Surrender	50-51
Lonely No More	52-53
One-Way	54-55
Testing of Your Faith	56-57
Lake Damascus	58-59
Social Gram	60-61
Walking the Walk	62-63
Mirror Image	64-65

Enemy Attack	66-67
It Is Finished	68-69
What's Next	70-71
Stand or Fall - The Choice Is Yours	72-73
Humility's Snare	74-75
Distracted Spirit	76-77
Decide to Abide and Reside	78-79
Joy's Journey	80-81
Meaningful Lives	82-83
Sharing Lights	84-85
I Am	86-87
Conclusion	88
I Am Because He Is	89

Finding a home is something that might seem so simple to most people, but not for me. I had not yet made it into recovery, and I had again fallen back into my reckless lifestyle and addictions. I lived far away from my children; I was very lonely, and I was trying to decipher what it all meant. It had been such a long time since I had a place to call home; so, I hoped that I could somehow keep hope alive and keep moving forward. My heart was in the right place, but because I was not truly following God's path for my life at the time, I always seemed to revert to old patterns to numb the pain. It became easier to medicate and to misbehave. I would drink, smoke pot, and go play poker—anything to distract my mind so I wouldn't think about the reality of my circumstances. What I realize now, after finding Christ, is that there is a home for everyone and that it's not anything we can see or touch. It is not of this world; it's about the next world and having faith to believe in things unseen. If you find yourself struggling to find your place in this world, a special and safe home, put your faith in Christ. He will guide you to where the water is always inviting and always warm.

> "Therefore we are always confident and know that as long as we are at home in the body we are away from the Lord. For we live by faith, not by sight. We are confident, I say, and would prefer to be away from the body and at home with the Lord. So we make it our goal to please him, whether we are at home in the body or away from it. For we must all appear before the judgment seat of Christ, so that each of us may receive what is due us for the things done while in the body, whether good or bad."
> — 2 Corinthians 5:6-10

Warm Waters

To many, the pond is home, filled with creatures and scenery well known,
These waters are familiar, they breathe easy through gills, and their seeds are sewn,

From generations of fabric, ancestors, grandparents, and yes…moms and dads,
They find their place in the pool; it becomes home, not temporary…never a fad.

A place of comfort, where their children play with the other fish with similar plights,
Learning to breathe, like the others, natural…without a struggle, without a fight.

But some fish leave the pool, either on their own, or with some of their kind,
Searching for warmer waters, not sure where they'll go or what they'll find.

They leave for fresher water, perhaps brighter and more colorful than the last,
Moving on, with the hope that these new pools will help them forget the past.

And they stay for a short while, still searching, not finding the right space,
Much of their time spent out of the water, gasping for air, a never-ending race.

To find a pool that is warm, friendly, and offers everything they seek,
But when they get there, for some reason, fear creeps in, and the pool starts to leak.

So, they jump out of the water, and quite often head back to whence they came,
But the old familiar waters have changed, the people in them; it's just not the same.

It doesn't feel right anymore, so again they leave, and their quest continues,
To find a home, somewhere that the water feels warm, and they still refuse;

To believe that there is a special pool for them, it just can't be; I must keep my faith,
God knows my struggles, my constant search; there must be a place;

That I can call home, where I can finally reside, free from fear and torment,
Where I can swim with ease, find comfort in the space, perhaps Heaven sent.

A place where all the fish I have met; close family, friends old and new,
Can find me, once and for all…the pain subsides…because I followed the clues.

While I searched, I had love and support from many searching for their own pool,
After all, we never really swim alone; we have people, God's grace, that's kind of cool.

This should give us strength to persevere, to never give up; it's worth the fight,
To find our warm waters, our place in the sea…that HOPE…that's our light!

I sat at my computer one morning trying to make sense of my life, wondering where all the time had gone. I pictured an hourglass; and a person (me) standing next to it just turning it over and over to get another chance—endeavoring to stop time, start over, to make things right. The concept of time was so difficult for me to grasp at that moment. It's interesting, because now that my faith is much stronger, I realize the truth of what I saw. I realize that in God's world, there is no time—a thousand years is like one day and one day is like a thousand years. Even while I was still struggling, God was always with me, somehow giving me a glimpse into the future. Looking back, I feel so blessed that God was patient enough to wait for me. Thank you, Lord. He will wait for you as well; He cares about YOU and has absolutely no connection to TIME.

Hourglass

I wonder what would happen if you took time away,
How would that affect your life, your nights, and your days?

Would you still worry about trivial matters and what needs to be accomplished?
Or would you rejoice, right now, in all the great things right in front of you?!

Because time does go by…yes…but it doesn't have to be such a deterrent,
If we learn to let go, rise above, and just flow with the ever-present current;

Of life, joy, peace, and love, what a blessing it would be to live so unencumbered,
You see, it's the effort that counts, not the result; this peace we seek is achievable.

If we have faith and truly believe that there's another life after this one,
Could we possibly ignore time, seize each day, and experience joy and fun?

Perhaps, but there's a gaping hole between writing the words and believing.
The reality is that our problems take over, people hurt us, and our faith diminishes.

But each new day brings hope and a light that "this too shall pass,"
And we each have an opportunity to fight through the adversity and ignore the hourglass.

Time, we can't control, things will change, we will grow older, and hopefully wiser.
This circle of life goes by so fast; it's up to us to slow down and pay more attention.

To our health, our families, our friends; to endeavor to make our mark,
On those we touch each day, if purposeful, our impact will be clear and stark.

And the time that controls our life can fade into the distant background,
While we elevate our lives, make time for others, and always stay positive!

"You gave me life and showed me kindness, and in your providence watched over my spirit."
— Job 10:12

It is such a comforting and beautiful feeling to know that God's hand was on me, even before I made it into rehab. I was still struggling, still gambling, still not near my kids. However, for some strange reason, I had the presence of mind to reach deep and pen the words that not only helped me get through these dark days, but words that reflect a belief in God's purpose for my life. Caught between pain and hope, I was still searching for comfort and a slot that felt right. I always knew there was a plan; I just didn't know that the only way to have it unfold was to relinquish everything to Christ. Now I know, and my prayer is that those who struggle with placement in their lives, feeling like they don't fit in anywhere, will realize that God made each one of us for a specific and special purpose.

> "I know your deeds, your love and faith, your service and perseverance, and that you are now doing more than you did at first."
> — Revelation 2:19

Where's the Fit

If it doesn't fit, then you must admit that there's another place,
Where you belong at this moment in time regardless of the pace.

You walk, jog, run, or sprint…. still searching for that perfect groove,
That you know must exist, so you try again, always willing to move;

To a new space, perhaps that is the answer, until you get there and it's still not right,
So, you buckle down, work hard, stay positive…never giving up the fight.

For your life, your career, your peace of mind, when did it all get so hard?
To live a normal, simple, and fulfilling life…. is it not in my cards?

Sure, it is, it's just not the right time, and the Man upstairs must have a plan,
So, you pray for providence and strength, trying to be the kind of man;

That your children, your family, and your friends will love and admire,
And you do your best to love yourself, an elusive goal, but something we all desire;

To actually FIT somewhere, with family, the right job, the right place to live,
Something that seems so simple, but our past mistakes make it hard to forgive;

Ourselves as we shed old skin, tread new waters trying to wash away the old ways,
But they seem to reappear when adversity creeps in, much to our dismay.

So, we continue to persevere, trusting in God, trying to believe it will all be OK,
Because there is a reason for everything that happens, at least that's what they say.

And deep down, you must believe that's true, I know I do, and that keeps me going,
Never losing my confidence, my core belief in myself, trusting in the ALL-KNOWING;

Man above who surely watches over me, my children, and everything in my life,
He knows we struggle, yet serves up free will, and when we falter, there will be strife;

That we must deal with, get through, and come out stronger on the other side,
In the end, it's how we deal with adversity that determines where we finally reside.

And the more I struggle, the more faithful I become, it's strange, but I must admit,
Trusting God's plan for me is winning the battle over trying to find a FIT.

Something everyone must love about Facebook is the birthday messages. On my 50th birthday, one of the folks that used to work for me wrote something so warm on my Facebook page; it brought me to tears. He told me that on this special day, those that love you come out and show you their love. What I realized at that moment is that throughout all my failures, indiscretions, and sinful living, my life was special. It was special because I truly have an abundance of love from so many people I've met over the years—especially my beloved children and family. Even though I was still in a bad place, this was a good day. In the end, it's all about legacy and eternity. I was reminded on this day that I have impacted many people and that I am important, even though I wasn't yet a friend to myself.

I dedicate this poem to all the amazing people pictured here.

Who You Have

The world gets small, and your heart gets large,
When you realize that you're the one in charge;

Of connecting with those important to you,
Family, friends, and others; you know it's true;

That this life is precious and short, and time is so valuable,
So, you do your best, press on, and attempt to be malleable;

As you meet new people and pave new paths each day,
Never losing sight of the ones you love; praying they stay;

With you on your journey, but you know it's up to you,
To keep them close, without using glue;

And the harder you try to forge these cherished bonds,
The larger your vessel becomes to help navigate the ponds;

Of life, my dear friends, as I bring this to close,
With these kinds words for all, tossed out in prose;

Because in the end, it's not what you have,
it's WHO YOU HAVE.

> "If I speak in the tongues of men or of angels, but do not have love, I am only a resounding gong or a clanging cymbal. If I have the gift of prophecy and can fathom all mysteries and all knowledge, and if I have a faith that can move mountains, but do not have love, I am nothing. If I give all I possess to the poor and give over my body to hardship that I may boast, but do not have love, I gain nothing. Love is patient, love is kind. It does not envy, it does not boast, it is not proud. It does not dishonor others, it is not self-seeking, it is not easily angered, it keeps no record of wrongs. Love does not delight in evil but rejoices with the truth. It always protects, always trusts, always hopes, always perseveres."
> — 1 Corinthians 13:1-7

Just before I entered rehab, I was at the dog track, waiting to get on a poker table. Yes, that's right. I was still in my gambling addiction, still writing about my confusing and spiraling life, and waiting to gamble my money away again. I thought maybe on this day I would win big. Everything would be OK. I was thinking about the animals — something that was unusual for me. I was sitting and looking out at the staging area for the dogs, where they prepare them for the race. This is where you play poker in Florida — at the dog track. How stupid we must look to them. Especially me, a man taking a few hundred dollars (I was small-time gambling at the time) to play a game with people I don't know, to win money, and to make myself feel better. However, even in my despair, The Lord was there — trying to show me that, even in this lonely and barren place, there was still hope for me. He showed me that I was strong enough to keep rising each time I fell.

In hindsight, this entire time was a perfect prelude for me to enter rehab. I was finally ready for The Lord to show me my way!!!

Chasing the Rabbit

Ever been to the dog track to see them race?
Around the sphere, chasing the fake rabbit at a furious pace.

The race ends, the animals rest…but not the anxious humans,
Some are happy, some are calm, but many are fuming;

Over not choosing the right dog, win, place, or show,
Not really thinking about the dogs, the silly path they take, do they really know?

What they are doing, why they are there…maybe they're the ones in the race,
Around their own circle…. of life…. always trying to chase;

Their own dreams, many attend to try and win and make money,
But only a few win anything, to me it seems funny;

That these dogs are bred, like horses, for human sport,
If they could talk, they would say, "These humans are all out of sorts."

For many of us, the circle seems endless, and the plight quite daunting,
And the rabbit we chase, although different for each, is constant and haunting.

As we try to find our place in the maze, facing trials, trying to overcome,
Enormous obstacles, and we wonder why it seems that some;

People get all of the breaks; I try hard, I believe, why is it that my race,
Has a strange similarity to the dogs, perpetual, regardless of the pace.

We try and keep while doing our best to make the right decisions,
On our journey through life, working hard to mend the incisions;

That we caused all on our own through the years, but on goes the pain,
So, we pray, we hustle; we continue to fight on, staying out of the rain.

And while the cloud seems to follow us, we stay faithful that the Lord sees ALL,
As our race continues, we must stay strong, focused, and rise each time we fall.

> "The Lord is my shepherd, I lack nothing. He makes me lie down in green pastures, he leads me beside quiet waters, he refreshes my soul. He guides me along the right paths for his name's sake. Even though I walk through the darkest valley, I will fear no evil, for you are with me; your rod and your staff, they comfort me."
> — Psalm 23:1-4

After a long night of playing poker and losing my last $500, I went home and cried myself to sleep. Fifty years old, away from my children, broke, and essentially homeless. I really didn't know what to do, so I called my Guardian Angels: **Marge & Mark Long**. Marge and Mark are dedicated children of God and missionaries that have spent their life serving The Lord. I knew, deep in my core, that God was the answer, and these were the most spiritually connected people I knew. It helped that Marge was also my baby sister. She and Mark did not hesitate to come to my rescue. After wrestling with them for several days about rehab and working through the painful conversations with my ex-wife and children, I reluctantly agreed to check into the year-long Christian-based recovery program at Fresh Start Ministries. My journey started with that first night in the 70-man facility — sleeping in my 8-man dorm. Scared, lonely, shameful, embarrassed, and full of self-doubt — my long-awaited process had begun.

Breaking the Chains

My first night in recovery was not very fun,
I didn't sleep a wink, except for the one;

Hour of shut-eye I was able to obtain,
While trying to overcome the guilt and the shame;

Why am I here? Is this the right place?
Or should I be trying something else just in case;

This doesn't work...wait...stop for a second and think,
You've tried everything else, perhaps there's a link;

Between your constant running and still feeling lost,
Fixing things yourself ...really, Tony? At what cost?

Maybe...just maybe it's time to let go and let God lead the way,
Your way doesn't work; it's time to just trust and to pray;

For strength, forgiveness, and definitely for God's grace,
Because He loves you so very much; and wants you to finish the race;

That He determined from the start, where your journey began,
But free will creeps in, the enemy grabs hold, but you know you still can;

Break the Chains of torment, insecurity, fear, guilt, and pain,
And finally surrender; come home to Him and step out of the rain.

"You have searched me, LORD, and you know me. You know when I sit and when I rise; you perceive my thoughts from afar. You discern my going out and my lying down; you are familiar with all my ways. Before a word is on my tongue you, LORD, know it completely."
— Psalm 139:1-4

*I dedicate this poem to
Lucas Brown; the counselor
who directed me on this special day.
May he rest in peace in the loving arms
of our Father.*

About a week into the program, I was starting to feel a little better about my decision to enter rehab, but I was still not quite ready to relinquish myself fully. That all changed on my 2nd Saturday in my new home—CHORE DAY. You see, the first 4 Saturdays in the program are designated chore days for the new clients entering the facility. I've never been one to spend time doing "deep cleaning" on anything, never mind what I was about to face. There was a young counselor that oversaw chores that day. I later found out that he was under specific directions to analyze each client and assign work that would identify how willing the client was to truly submit to the rules and the discipline required for successful recovery. I must admit, I was blind-sided by this one—especially when he called my name and asked me to get a scrub brush, a bucket, and to meet him in the kitchen. He then gave me directions on how to clean the caked-on grease off the legs of the fryer. My immediate reaction was to tell him, "No way! Do you know who I am?" But instead, I decided to accept the challenge and got down on my hands and knees to work.

This is where I met The Lord, and this is where I fully surrendered for the first time in my life. I heard it loud and clear, directly from The Almighty: "This is where we do this, Tony. Right here, right now." I was overcome with emotion but didn't want the other guys to see me crying. I kept my head down and proceeded to scrub those legs for about 30 minutes straight—until they were shining bright! It was the most humbling experience of my entire life; and as soon as I was complete, I felt an amazing rush of adrenaline from The Holy Spirit. I had never felt so empowered, and I thought to myself, "OK, I can do this."

Right Here... Right Now

The day started early as we reluctantly entered the dining hall, ready to work.
I was anxious and unsettled, knowing that I was in this setting because I acted like a jerk.

A self-fulfilling prophecy, I knew that my selfish ways would eventually lead me to my knees.
But not this way, cleaning caked-on grease off the fryer? Really? My first reaction was to freeze.

Can I accomplish this task, do I even know how, or will I embarrass myself trying?
But I soon realized that no one was watching me, except my Savior, and I started crying.

Weeping uncontrollably while I worked hard on my task, hearing a message loud and clear,
"This is where we do this." He said to me; "Let go; step out of the boat, and I will steer;

You to safety, to the life you were meant to live, the one I designed for you from the start,
And surrendering everything to Me is where it all begins, *and together* you and I will chart;

The course for your future, to repent and turn the other way, no more striving, no more strife,
Finally realizing that **the pursuit to become who you were meant to be is the secret to life.**

It's never been about the destination; once you come to Me your eternity becomes certain,
No more worry, wading in self-pity, wondering where you stand; because behind the curtain."

There is nothing; no hidden mystery, everything you need is inside of you in your perfect design,
As long as The Lord leads your life and you start walking His way, you can now start to align;

With the righteous path that accompanies your destiny; now believing in things unseen,
Be still and rest in this premise; because your conscience is like a soft pillow when it's clean.

> "Therefore, since we are surrounded by such a great cloud of witnesses, let us throw off everything that hinders and the sin that so easily entangles. And let us run with perseverance the race marked out for us, fixing our eyes on Jesus, the pioneer and perfecter of faith. For the joy set before him he endured the cross, scorning its shame, and sat down at the right hand of the throne of God."
> — Hebrews 12:1-2

During my first few weeks in rehab, I was able to get a job but didn't have a car. Actually, I had a car coming into the facility, but I was way behind on payments, and the car was in my mother's name. After submitting to God and to the program, I decided to finally make a good financial decision and turn in the car. One morning, I drove to the bank, dropped off the car, and walked 3 miles down the street to work. I felt good about that decision, mostly because my mother would no longer get calls from the bank on my behalf. I was already feeling better about myself, and that afternoon, I decided I would take the bus home. Well, my first attempt at taking the bus was a failure. I stood on the wrong side of the street and missed the bus completely. I was able to call another brother from the ministry to come get me, and I sat down to wait for him to pick me up. I think I was just figuring out that the true gifts in life were hidden on the lower shelves, not on the higher shelves.

Treasure Map

The elusive X marks the spot where all the treasure is hidden,
And finding and hitting that mark is foreign to us, almost forbidden.

We imagine it's not for us; we don't deserve gifts, and how can it be?
That God waits for us to seek Him; yes, that means you and even me.

Gifts we can only uncover if we straighten up and change our ways,
And follow our Lord God who knows full well our troubled nights and days.

Lives unfulfilled, chasing material things that we all think we deserve,
While the enemy, ever-present, lingers, and encourages us to pursue and preserve;

Our legacy through what we do, what we have, and what others will think,
When all of the sudden, we realize that we are way off course, and we start to sink;

Into a pool of despair, self-pity, fear, worry, and undeniable pain,
And the guy down south just smiles with pride while we just complain;

About our lives, our mistakes, our trials, where did we go off track?
We were so close to the hidden treasure, but now we feel an attack;

Of the heart, the spirit, the body, how can we ever begin to recover?
But then we find God, who is always there, and He can help us like no other;

Material thing, person, or feeling we can get from this broken earth,
And we start to breathe again; He fills us with love, like it was at our birth.

When he made is in His own perfect image, with our own incredible and unique style,
And our beautiful treasure comes back into view, complete with a smile.

"Therefore I tell you, do not worry about your life, what you will eat or drink; or about your body, what you will wear. Is not life more than food, and the body more than clothes? Look at the birds of the air; they do not sow or reap or store away in barns, and yet your heavenly Father feeds them. Are you not much more valuable than they? Can any one of you by worrying add a single hour to your life? "And why do you worry about clothes? See how the flowers of the field grow. They do not labor or spin. Yet I tell you that not even Solomon in all his splendor was dressed like one of these. If that is how God clothes the grass of the field, which is here today and tomorrow is thrown into the fire, will he not much more clothe you—you of little faith? So do not worry, saying, 'What shall we eat?' or 'What shall we drink?' or 'What shall we wear?' For the pagans run after all these things, and your heavenly Father knows that you need them. But seek first his kingdom and his righteousness, and all these things will be given to you as well. Therefore do not worry about tomorrow, for tomorrow will worry about itself. Each day has enough trouble of its own."
— Matthew 6:25-34

During the beginning stages of recovery, each night we attended classes that were part of our orientation. We would talk about a recovery topic, about our addictions, and typically add in some Bible study and healthy dialogue where everyone could participate. Many of the men in our program had some deep-rooted family issues, particularly concerning their fathers. One night, while talking about forgiveness, one of the men shared a story about the time his father was just about to throw acid on his mother. He reacted quickly, stepped in front of his mother, and the acid went all over his body. He showed us the scars while tears flowed down his face. We were all moved. One by one, each of the men shared a similar childhood experience. I started to feel something in the room, but I had no idea what it was. All I know is that I started to sweat and was completely overwhelmed with emotion. I didn't share anything that night, but one man closed the session with a horrifying story about something that happened to him when he was a small child. He endured terrible abuse, yet through his tears, he finished his story by saying the following: "How could I NOT forgive my father? Look at what Christ did for me on the cross." I was in shock, my body started shaking, and I wept uncontrollably for about 30 minutes. Later. I realized what I had been feeling was the Holy Spirit, literally my first real-time experience with this awesome part of our Triune God.

Rocked by Paul

The class started out normal; like any other,
Until we started talking about life: about fathers and mothers.

Several guys stood up and offered tear-jerking testimonies,
Real men, suffering, arduously confessing, spilling out their guts; definitely not phony.

Just a broken band of brothers all recovering from their own type of addictions,
Trying to make sense of it all while dealing with stress & contradiction.

Battles within our hearts and minds; deep wounds and scars from the past,
But somehow telling stories in fellowship helped each one of us cast;

Out our individual nets of protection while seeking God's grace,
And then, all of the sudden, out of nowhere, I got smacked on the face;

By a Mack truck disguised as a Rock,
And the words from this young man captivated me, and put me in shock.

The shock turned to tears and they just kept flowing,
As he spewed out his story about how our All-Knowing;

Father sent His only Son down to die for us and to save us ALL,
And regardless of what we face, if we trust and believe, he will never let us fall;

Into despair, even though we will experience excruciating and unforgettable pain,
He helps us forgive, move on, so we can finally step out of the rain.

Finally, we can start living the life he planned for us ALL,
And on this special night, our God chose to REMIND US through Paul.

"Then Peter came to Jesus and asked, 'Lord, how many times shall I forgive my brother or sister who sins against me? Up to seven times?' Jesus answered, 'I tell you, not seven times, but seventy-seven times.'"
— Matthew 18:21-22

Father's Day was a hard day for me. You see, when I first surrendered to God in the program, I started to feel good about my direction. Every day, God was giving me new strength to walk straight and to move forward. But certain things hit me extra hard my first few months, and Father's Day without my kids was rough! It was an incredibly sad day as I sat out on the dock with my iPhone. Usually, we were not allowed to have our phones on Sunday, but they let us have them for a few hours that day. I was able to call my children to let them know how much I loved them and that I would be home as soon as I was able. Imagine the pain…

*I dedicate this poem to my amazing five children:
AJ, Austin, Alexander, Andersen, and Annalise.*

Father's Day

My first Father's Day without my beautiful kids,
A stark reminder of my fall and my well-chronicled skid.

A valley of darkness, despair; but I'm now finding hope,
In a place of recovery from gambling, alcohol, and dope.

Addictions that have affected my life and the lives of so many,
But trusting God in the valley helps us recover and provides fuel for any;

Challenges we may face, and although we will certainly struggle,
If we are faithful to Him, we will...once again...get to snuggle;

With our precious children; and this time it will be enhanced,
Because in rehab, we re-opened and then healed our wounds in attempt to advance;

Our ability to live life less prideful; with greater strength and humility,
So, our children can now see us strong and steady, no longer a victim of self-pity.

And our future Father's Day celebrations will far outweigh the past,
When we were too busy, wrapped up in ourselves, it all went by so fast.

Now is the time to let go and finally get true guidance and wisdom from above,
We know our way does not work; it's time to shift gears; it's time we try love.

Because love makes it all work, and if we put our faith where it belongs,
Next year will be different if we trust and believe; we'll be singing new songs.

"Start children off on the way they should go, and even when they are old they will not turn from it."
— Proverbs 22:6

One Saturday morning in June, I decided I would walk to downtown Orlando. It was about an hour-long walk through a nice part of town. When I got there, I grabbed a sandwich and sat down by the lake. I was listening to worship music. It was Christian pop music that I learned to love early in the program. I sat there watching the animals, the people, and looking at the tall buildings downtown, and an unbelievable feeling of peace came over me. I knew it was directly from God because I can't remember ever being so completely quiet and still—just me and The Lord, sitting there, listening to music, having some lunch, and enjoying the scenery. I had never really been one to appreciate the small things in life, but that has changed. Thank you, Lord.

Peace

I've recently captured a peaceful and wonderful feeling that permeates my skin.
My Lord and Savior has filled me with hope, joy, and love…He's forgiven my sins.
The journey is just beginning, but I'm walking straighter and standing taller.
My heart is softening, my tears are flowing, and it's all because I'm now a caller;

Upon my Father, who reigns supreme, His omnipresence gives me strength to win the daily fight;
Over the enemy who knows me all too well, this guy with horns used to haunt me day and night.

The evil one is angry that he's lost one of his pals; his tactics are now more thought out and clever,
But the battle gets easier each day. I'm stronger, more equipped, and now I can find the lever;

That can be pulled when temptation creeps in and tries to catch me asleep at the wheel,
I quickly awaken, read the Word, get lost in prayer…and emerge with an armor of steel.

With shield in hand, love in my heart, knowledge, and new wisdom in between my ears,
I'm able to tackle any obstacle, not by myself anymore, but with God…the One who truly hears;

All of our prayers, and if we come to Him always and NOT just when things are bad,
He will lift your spirit, work on your heart, and you'll spend way more time happy than sad.

And a PEACE will come over you, it has for me, and although it doesn't last all day,
It sure beats the days when I walked alone, without Jesus, often caught up in the fray;

Of a life undirected, double-minded, prideful, and sinful. Most of the time I felt like a fraud.
No…I think I'll take this path, the one I'm on now, the one less traveled, paved for me perfectly by my God.

> "And the peace of God, which transcends all understanding, will guard your hearts and your minds in Christ Jesus."
> — Philippians 4:7

July 4, 2013, was the day I made a public profession of my faith in Christ and got baptized. Fresh Start Ministries always has a huge party on the 4th of July, and many alumni and family members attend. In hindsight, I wish that my kids had been there, but I could not navigate that so early on in my program. Forty broken men, all struggling from some type of addiction, went into the lake that day to be baptized. While I stood with Pastor Tim and Pastor Joe, I was again driven to tears by the magnitude of what was happening. After I came out of the water, I felt so good, so proud, and so completely RIGHT. After living so many years WRONG, it just felt incredible!! AMEN!!

I dedicate this poem to Pastor Tim Carlsward and Pastor Joe Cordovano, the two great men who run this amazing ministry. Love you guys.

Submerged

The water was dirty, but the smiles were bright,
As forty men prepared to step into the light;

Of a kingdom so special, so pure, it was hard to contain,
The overwhelming joy, for the moment, outweighed all of the guilt and the pain.

For the many years of abuse to our bodies, our minds, and all those we love,
For the day was filled with promise, hope, and a new life from above.

From a God who is patient, He doesn't want to, but He will wait until we are ready,
To be healed, born again, and to live our lives strong and steady.

To live our life's purpose, our God given assignment if you will,
Without having to rely on ourselves, money, booze, and pills.

Once and for all we come alive with our outward profession; we rejoice and sing,
Because before this, we were all saved by committing our lives and hearts to the one true King.

A God who will help us navigate the unchartered waters,
And those of us with children are now able to show our sons and our daughters;

What it means to be a Christian, to let go and let Him lead the way,
And our lives will be enhanced, we can finally start living, we'll start each morning with a ray;

Of sunshine, anticipating each moment with new promise that is sure to unfold,
Because we chose to **SUBMERGE**, to get baptized, now our real stories can be told.

"And this water symbolizes **baptism** that now saves you also—not the removal of dirt from the body but the pledge of a clear conscience toward God. It saves you by the resurrection of Jesus Christ."
— 1 Peter 3:21 (emphasis mine)

Humility was never really a strong suit for me. I lived so many years with an oversized ego; it was extremely hard to be truly authentic and humble. As I mentioned, at the beginning of the program, I made the difficult decision to turn in my car. Therefore, I had to get to work each day, and my office was about 15 miles away. Now keep in mind, I am from New York, but I grew up on Eastern Long Island. I really didn't have much experience with public transportation. It was quite a challenge for me initially, but over time, I learned to appreciate the experience. In fact, I started to enjoy it, and as my faith was growing, I was able to meet and share with many people that I would have never met if I had not been riding the bus each day. One day, I was riding home from work and had a flashback to high school when we used to take the bus to all of the great sports events — a good memory. When my mind flashed back to the present, I was overwhelmed with the growth that God had bestowed upon my heart and upon my life.

> "Therefore, as God's chosen people, holy and dearly loved, clothe yourselves with compassion, kindness, **humility**, gentleness, and patience."
> — Colossians 3:12 (emphasis mine)

Back on the Bus

In my younger years, the bus was yellow and the ride enjoyable, I don't ever remember feeling out of sorts,
We rode back and forth to school, on field trips, and many.... many times,...to play sports.

Those times were especially exciting, with a rush of adrenaline and anticipation to play the games we loved.
But today I'm on the bus because I've lost my car, and many other things, all because I let the enemy in; until he pushed, and he shoved;

Me to the point where I not only lost my possessions; I let my loved ones down,
And the bus, until a few weeks ago anyway, was a stark reminder of the consequences of my actions, and I traveled with a frown.

I was separated from God, unfulfilled; my life was truly out of control,
And the shame and guilt lead me to depression, low self-esteem, with no hope for my soul.

Until just recently when I prayed for God to enter my heart and direct my much-needed recovery,
And riding the bus today, with a new heart, I seem to have clear discernment for discovery.

With renewed purpose for my life, a shield in my hand, and humility in my bones,
The Holy Spirit rides with me now, and even though I'm not used to public transportation, I'm no longer alone.

The old me would ride alongside these people with an intolerant attitude; in some sort of fog,
But now I know they are all children of God, some don't even know it, and I find myself seeking out new dialog;

With those I encounter, from all walks of life; and regardless of their plight,
Our God never leaves us, He wants us to come home, and He wants us to fight;

For the strength to live out our assignment, our purpose, it's available for each and every one of us,
And now I'm taking a new and purposeful route, and I thank my God for putting me *Back on the Bus*.

Out by the water, at the ministry, there is a huge wooden cross in the water. I spent quite a bit of time praying and laying down my pain, suffering, resentment, and anger at the foot of that cross. I enjoyed the peace and solitude on the dock and my many moments alone with God in that serene setting I will never forget. One particular day, I was praying and found myself staring at my reflection in the water. It was a moving and inspirational moment. More like, "Wow, I am really changing."

"For now we see only a **reflection** as in a mirror; then we shall see face to face. Now I know in part; then I shall know fully, even as I am fully known."
— 1 Corinthians 13:12 (emphasis mine)

Face to Face by Water's Edge

All our lives, we've tried to hide and outrun ourselves,
From truth, reality, and many of life's treasures hidden on the lower shelves.

Afraid to face the mirror, we don't like what we see, so we choose the easy road,
The path to self-comfort, medicated realities, typically avoiding the heavy load;

That we carry deep inside while we try and numb the pain,
Our lives move forward, until we fall again; and then we must explain;

To our family and friends; our lies, our deception, and our reasons for hiding,
Behind the towering walls we set up to AVOID, temporarily anyway, the inevitable sliding;

Into the abyss, where the pain and suffering finally gets to the point,
Where we land somewhere, a place where we can't find extra money, a beer, or a joint;

To numb our pain and run from our horrifying circumstances,
No more lies, no more excuses, no more hiding or taking chances.

For reasons yet uncovered, it's different in each case,
God placed us by the **Water's Edge** to come **Face to Face**;

With our demons, our addictions, and all of the things that caused us to run,
Because our Lord has plans for us, and we've landed where there's more work and less fun.

He knows our purpose, and through Him we are learning new skills,
Authentic and practical lessons, through His word, and we now get chills;

Down our spine and feelings like we've never felt before,
Peace, joy, LOVE, and a comfort level that makes us all yearn for more;

Of God's love, we come alive; fellowship with one another, and we start to care;
For EVERYONE in our path, old and new, because we are NOW equipped to SHARE.

Phase II of the program required us to dive deep and uncover where we went wrong through the process of inner healing. Some of the stories I heard about the upbringing of some of these young men made me feel unworthy to be in recovery with them. I sometimes felt so unbelievably shameful. I had it all, and the majority of my downfall was self-inflicted. These kids were abused, left behind, imprisoned, orphaned, doing drugs with their dads at incredibly young ages—it was horrifying. But, I soon realized that this was no accident. I was there at this exact time for a specific reason. This process would unfold over time, but the opportunity to help some of these kids was one of the most rewarding experiences of my life. I learned so much about myself through this process, and I am eternally grateful for the entire Phase II process.

Unbearable Pain No More

How can we bear the pain as a result of the damages we've left behind?
When the enemy wedged in and controlled most of our thoughts; infiltrating our minds;

The wake of destruction is often devastating, mostly for the ones we were closest to.
And the waves left seem perpetual, so we try and change ourselves; as well as quite a few;

Of our damaging behavior patterns, bad habits, and harmful addictions,
While we attempt to face reality, usually alone, and despite our afflictions;

We try to move on, but soon realize that our own best thinking is what landed is in this barren and fruitless place,
And the **unbearable pain** gets worse, until we surrender, come home to God, and He begins to erase;

All of the hurt in our hearts; we begin to pray, and eventually start to believe and trust,
That God sent His one and only son to die for our sins, so we now know that we must;

Continue to move toward the light, and keep our faith in Him and things unseen,
Because our lives cannot be fulfilled without God in control; He will make us clean.

And our pain gets washed away; we are no longer afraid, no longer broken,
We begin to understand Jesus, His love, the Bible, and the words that were spoken;

By our Father in Heaven, the One who can make all of the pain and suffering go away,
All because we submit, we now let Him lead, and He brightens our darkest days.

"My comfort in my **suffering** is this: Your promise preserves my life."
— Psalm 119:50 (emphasis mine)

One night, we had a lesson on codependency, and it was fascinating to me. Not because I had others in my life that were codependent with me, but because I was actually codependent with myself. I had developed a dangerous pattern of behavior that allowed me to take credit for purposefully doing good things. In reality, the sole reason for doing those things was to make myself feel better for the ridiculously sinful life I was living. Yes, that's right. I would write pieces to get accolades. I would help people just because they would give me credit for helping them, and I would look good. I would make up stories of how successful I was, so people could tell me how great I was. It was awful; I was awful. This lesson brought this home for me, and I am so thankful I recognized the habit-forming behavior I had used as a lubricant to continue to misbehave. Thank you, Lord, for showing me this so clearly; I am free!!!

"Then you will know the truth, and the truth will set you free."
— John 8:32

Codependency's Foe

Ever sit back and wonder why you do certain things?
Why you feel compelled to rely on the past and pull the same strings;

We are like puppet masters, trying so desperately to navigate our lives,
But the enemy is clever, he manipulates, and never uses forks or spoons; just knives.

While he surgically cuts his way into our preoccupied minds,
We become easy targets; we give up, and believe that we are the kinds;

Of people who need approval from everyone for everything,
Negotiating our own terms, until each circumstance begins to have a familiar ring.
A resounding melody of old and worn out habits,
To ensure everyone likes us, we need approval; we even pull the same rabbits;

Out of our tattered hats, but our eyes eventually open, and we can finally see,
That all we are doing is repeating the past and befriending codependency.

But until we wake up and seek new wisdom from our one true source,
It's really difficult to set our sails, right our ships, and get back on course.

The course that God has set for our lives, our purpose, and our legacy,
As we shed the need for approval, accolades, I know this is true for me.

And now I'm seeing, believing, and trusting that the only way to be whole,
Is to seek approval from my Savior, not from people; only He can purify my soul.

I dedicate this poem to Lynn Dykes, the founder of the SWAT team. May he rest in peace at home with our Lord and Savior.

A few weeks into the program, one of my brothers invited me to join them on the dock on Sunday evening for some quiet prayer time and fellowship. I was eager to fix my life, so the invitation was welcome. Those meetings became such a huge part of my recovery — working through issues with each other, and we had so many memorable moments simply sharing life. It was amazing, and soon others started to join. We decided to give the group a name.

The Fresh Start "SWAT" team:
S - Sanctified
W - Warriors
A - At
T - Twilight

"For our struggle is not against flesh and blood, but against the rulers, against the authorities, against the powers of this dark world and against the **spiritual** forces of evil in the heavenly realms."
— Ephesians 6:12 (emphasis mine)

The Fresh Start "S.W.A.T." Team

It all started out so innocently, unplanned, but the placid lake was calling,
On a Sunday night in January with just a few chosen men; broken and tired of falling;

On their faces. They started out simple, talking about life, each sharing their own tragic plight,
The winds kicked up, the temperature dropped, but it was still a whimsical and beautiful night;

Brothers in arms, recovering from addiction, not really knowing what to say or what to expect,
But The Lord knew this was not just a chance meeting at the dock, this was the moment and time to elect;

The inaugural Fresh Start SWAT Team, empowered by God, for deliberate purposes not yet known,
These three would soon become four, five, and six, and that night — the initial seeds were sown.

Seeds that would grow into lasting friendships, support, and non-judgmental love,
And these Warriors became stronger; they opened up to each other; this pleased the Lord above.

They began to realize that this was special and definitely part of God's plan; and others would certainly follow,
Because what they see are clear and stark changes in the men from the dock, they seem peaceful and no longer wallow;

In self-pity, depression, shame, and unrelenting pain and regret,
Their guilt has withered by the lake, and The Lord now equips them with a large and secure net.

Designed to catch others who are also struggling with their past mistakes; unclean and impure,
The serene setting and silhouettes offer safe haven for new Warriors with an aesthetic lure;

That draws men in to join this team; as they each open up and tell their own stories of pain and regret,
But the stories quickly turn to praise for God, their hearts **also** change; and they are now set;

To pick up their weapons and don their suit of armor; feeling strong and empowered to serve,
No more worry about things they can't control; sanctified by Christ, now blessed with the nerve:

To stand up for what's right, not follow the crowd; now is the time to learn and to share,
The wisdom they gain from each other through the Holy Spirit, these recovering Warriors begin to care;

For others, not just themselves anymore, and their lives now make sense; the truth is finally revealed,
Because they were chosen by The Lord to join this band of brothers, and their eternity is now sealed.

In all honesty, I always knew that I was on the wrong path. I never had the courage to look deep within myself and identify my purpose for living this life. I was way too busy trying to make money, get praise, and show everyone how great I was. I had so much clarity in Phase II of the program; I did a tremendous amount of writing. Expressing myself through words is very cathartic for me, and somehow writing poetry and rhyming serves a similar purpose as perhaps a metronome does for a musician. I feel like I have a *"shell"* when I write poetry. Once I get inspired by a message that I wish to convey, the words just flow. One night before dinner, I sat on my own out at the dock. I finally felt like my life had meaning again; I was right where I needed to be.

Clarity's Purpose at the Lake

I always knew, deep in my soul, that I was not following the right path,
That I was fooling everyone; but somehow I knew that I would eventually feel the wrath;

For my bad behaviors and poor decisions, way too many to count,
My best thinking lead me to worship idols, acquire possessions; there was never an amount;

Too large for me to consider; no risk I was unwilling to take,
To prove how smart and cool I was, how much I could gather; a self-created fake;

Person; living life by his own rules; in an ego-centric and perpetual motion,
Until my lens came into focus; when I finally realized that all of this confusion and commotion;

Wasn't really necessary; the stress can truly leave my soul; there IS another way,
There is a Lord and Savior who has already paid the price for me; now there's a new ray;

Of sunshine that fills my heart; a new lamp at my feet,
Now I can walk both in the darkness and in the light; I feel absolutely complete;

With a new purpose for my life, redeemed by the Power of God,
I'm starting to live the life He intended for me, and none of this feels odd;

Just natural; I've been thirsty for this type of peace the entire time,
But my flesh was weak, not so much anymore; now it's much easier for me to rhyme;

The words I write on paper with a new and authentic flare,
Inspired by the Word of God, I'm now completely aware;

That this way, God's way; is definitely the path I should take,
Clarity's Purpose takes on new meaning for me, coming into crystal clear view at the Lake.

> "Once more Jesus put his hands on the man's eyes. Then his eyes were opened, his sight was restored, and he saw everything **clearly**."
> — Mark 8:25 (emphasis mine)

One Saturday in late July, I had the privilege of finally getting back on the golf course. I played with some of the guys from work, and we had a great time. I was calm, peaceful, and my golf game seemed to follow suit; I played a very nice round of golf. I was so appreciative and thankful for this simple pleasure that I hadn't taken part in…in quite some time. On the way home from playing golf with my co-workers, I was looking in the car mirror and read the notice, "Objects in the rear-view mirror are larger than they appear." I started thinking about forgiving myself for the horror of my past and realized it was all about perspective. The items from my past can get smaller if I just walk the right path. You see, there is no condemnation for those who are in Christ. Something I was reminded of that day.

Objects in the Rear-View Mirror Are "Smaller" Than They Appear

Why does our past haunt us to the point where we can't forget,

All of our mistakes, our shortcomings; our worries and regrets?

As we fight and struggle to find an opening in our self-made cocoon,

We stay hidden in our lies, justifications, and excuses; but soon;

We come to realize that we inevitably have a hard choice to make,

Should we stay here, unhappy, trapped inside our flesh, until we eventually break?

Or do we begin to trust in God, surrender, and turn our problems over to Him once and for all,

Because through Christ all things are possible; He can renew and strengthen us, and help us break our fall;

And He reminds us that the objects in our Rear-View Mirrors have no attachment to His Love and to His Grace,

Yes, there are circumstances; but we will overcome those, move on, and eventually find our place;

In the Kingdom of God, not because of anything we've done; not a win or a loss,

But because of what our Father did for us, sending His only son to die for our sins... on a cross.

> "Therefore, there is now no **condemnation** for those who are in Christ Jesus."
> — Romans 8:1 (emphasis mine)

One night during Phase II, one of my brothers in the program talked about some deep problems of the past. He was getting "processed" by one of the counselors, which was a deep line of questioning specifically geared for purposes of honesty and recovery. This particular counselor had such great insight into this young man's plight that I found myself lost within the moment, and The Holy Spirit took over the room. After a long and arduous effort and dialogue between the two, the struggling addict had a major breakthrough—realizing that God was there and had always been. He was overwhelmed with relief, joy, and love that His Savior had already paid the price and that he no longer had to suffer. He was covered by a peace and he mentioned that he knew Grace had saved him. I was making notes the entire time…

Grace

We hear the word, but how many truly know what it means?
Grace, it sounds so regal, how do WE get that; when our lives fall apart at the seams;

It must be for the spiritual people who live life the right way; don't you see?
After all, I'm a sinner; caught up in a spider web personally weaved by me;

All my years of inauthentic living; selfishly feeding my worldly flesh,
But somehow God still seeks me; His ultimate desire is to mesh;

His unconditional love and my acceptance; could this really be true?
That I still have a chance at a fulfilling life; no longer sad, lonely, and blue;

And the Joy that comes from God's Amazing Grace sets in; how sweet the sound,
That saved a wretch like me, and you, and him, and her...yes...even her;
His mercy knows no bounds.

Grace comes in the form of favor that cannot be earned and we don't deserve,
But asking God to come in your heart and lead your life is all it takes to be born again and to reserve;
Your spot in Heaven; yes, that's right; that means life eternal,
Once you decide this path, peace enters your heart, directly from your paternal;

Creator that sent His only son so we can have this so-called elusive Grace,
We can ALL have it; our tree starts bearing good fruit; and we are back in the race;

To the end, now sanctified by the Holy Spirit How cool is that?
Now we must walk in out, it's not easy, but we are now able to combat;

The enemy, who will elevate his desire to bring us down once again.
But our God will protect us, He will give us armor; He knows how it all began.

He also knows where it ends, and if we trust His Word and His love in every case,
Our lives will be enhanced while we are here; because our heart will be covered with Grace.

> "For it is by **grace** you have been saved, through faith—
> and this is not from yourselves, it is the gift of God."
> — Ephesians 2:8 (emphasis mine)

One of the true blessings of being at Fresh Start was that everything started to change as soon as I decided to surrender. While I was in Phase II, I was frustrated with some of my brothers who had not made that decision yet. I could see the lack of growth as a result. I spent a great deal of time (and still do) pressing into these young men to see if I could help. My goal was to communicate that although God will always love you and seek you, you must do your part to receive his full blessings and favor for your life. The Bible refers to this as the division of labor. It all starts with surrender, and I was thankful that The Lord showed me that very quickly when I entered the program.

"He himself bore our sins" in his body on the **cross**, so that we might die to sins and live for righteousness; "by his wounds you have been healed."
— 1 Peter 2:24 (emphasis mine)

Surrender

What visions come to mind when you hear this word?
Are they visions of war, prison, losing a fight? Haven't you heard?

That true surrender can be far more positive and even uplifting,
And for some of us in recovery; the word provides a new hope; no more sifting;

Through the quagmire of weeds and thorns that choke our momentum until we stop growing,
We think we have it all figured out After all, we have made it this far: just by knowing;

What to do, where to go, how to behave, and ultimately what to believe,
But when we do things our own way, we quite often lose our way and eventually we leave;

To try something new; only to find out that we still need help; we are still lost,
But there is always hope; if we search, our Lord can find us, and we can stop getting sauced;

On alcohol, drugs, and other damaging and habit-forming addictions,
We finally admit that we've lost control; our lives have become a contradiction;

Between how God made us and how we are walking; maybe it's time to try His plan,
Predetermined from the start; His loving arms stay open, and He still can;

Help change the course of our lives; we surrender; we repent,
We come alive, our hearts change, we have peace; and now we know that we were meant;

To do something special with our God-given talents and skills,
We can make an impact on others, a significant imprint that will give us chills;

Just to think about how much He cares for and loves us; our SURRENDER was the start,
Of our lives renewed; refreshed; we now feel empowered to chart;

Our new and purposeful course on our journey around this crazy sphere,
With God at the helm, we are given life eternal, and favor while we're still here.

Another powerful exercise we encountered in Phase II of the program was the breaking of *"soul ties"* with people from our past. This was a very painful and difficult process for many men, and I was no exception. We evaluated all the relationships we had in the past and came to terms with the mistakes we made through those relationships. Going through lists of people from my past during this process gave me a very lonely and empty feeling, but it had to be done. I had lost so many people and so much of myself over the years, mostly because I was feeding my flesh and not walking a straight path. However, what God showed me during this process was truly life-changing. Now, I don't feel as lonely because I know He is always there. And the more I walk closely to Him, the more rewarding my life becomes.

"So do not fear, for I am with you; do not be dismayed, for I am your God.
I will strengthen you and help you; I will uphold you with my righteous right hand."
— Isaiah 41:10

Lonely No More

Loneliness can be an exhausting, painful, and reoccurring experience,
Especially for those of us who chase idols, we always seem to be straddling the fence.

We live life on the edge, taking unnecessary, unusual, and even dangerous chances,
When all we have to do is slow down, get quiet, trust in God; regardless of the plight or circumstances;

We face in our battle to forgive ourselves of our past sins and indiscretions,
Those things that cause loneliness in the first place; but in the wake, there are poignant lessons;

That we can learn from as we align ourselves with like-minded people; other believers,
People who can help us face our challenges; together; we begin to ignore the deceivers;

That so often occupied our time and our minds; We got tied in knots; and thought; if only,
We could stay on the right path, let God lead; would we no longer be lonely?

Could we really escape that miserable life where we felt frozen and held captive?
By our past, our plight, what others thought about us; surely we're more adaptive;

Than we think we are; if we only knew where to run, and who to turn to in our desperate hour,
Of need; then we see, **YES**, there is hope; it lies in God's love, grace, and His ultimate power;

And our loneliness can subside; trust me; this works; it really can,
I can attest first hand; I'm doing it now; and I'm finally becoming the man;

God intended when my script was written while residing in my mother's womb,
Now I no longer feel lonely, all because Jesus died and escaped the tomb.

And my life now makes sense again; there is hope and a clear and bright future,
For me, my children, I can now start to heal and sew up the suture;

Left from the wounds of my past, I am forgiven, redeemed, and finally free,
Never alone again, I have a Savior, and there is not a chance that He will EVER leave.

One morning, while I was walking from the bus stop to work, I noticed a sign on the road. Actually, there were four signs all strategically placed together. The four signs were: *One Way, No Left Turn, Wrong Way,* and *No U-Turn.* I thought, *"WOW, thank you, Lord."* You see, once you are walking in The Lord's light and headed in the right direction, there is really only ONE WAY to go!

One-Way

On my route to work, I noticed four signs strategically placed together,
When I took a second glance, something happened, and I wondered whether;

Or not; these signs were placed there just for me; could it be? I'm sure they were now,
Because the four signs had a distinct message and a direct correlation as to how;

I am trying to live my life, doing the next right thing; now I'm on a new path,
Because my old life, led by me, was not going well; and I was feeling the wrath;

Of a sinful existence, following the crowd and feeding my demons and desires,
Until the sand in the hourglass was empty on top; I was lost, lonely, and even my wires;

Were crossed and all jacked up, I had no idea what to do or which way to turn,
Should I go back, to the left, in through the OUT-DOOR; I was unable to discern.

But not anymore; my messages are more vivid, purposeful, and crystal clear,
God captains my ship now; I just follow his lead because I know He's always near.

He hears and answers my prayers; as long as I walk tall and walk straight,
I can now be part of the crowd that obtains favor; the ones who pass through the narrow gate;

That leads to eternal life; what an awesome feeling; I can honestly and truly say,
"I'm wearing my armor proud" because I've figured it out — there is only ONE WAY!!

"Enter through the **narrow gate.** For wide is the **gate** and broad is the road that leads to destruction, and many enter through it. But small is the **gate** and **narrow** the road that leads to life, and only a few find it."
— Matthew 7:13-14 (emphasis mine)

As we entered Phase III of the program, I felt that I was truly growing spiritually. My job was going great, my relationships were improving, and life seemed to be getting back on track. However, there was part of the program that I found extremely challenging: drug testing. Unlike many guys in the program, I wasn't programmed to go to the bathroom with someone standing in the room. Also, I had no issue with hard drugs, and no way could I test positive. It was an ego and non-compliance issue, certainly something that has haunted me for years. The guys in the program used to get a kick out of my displeasure during this process, but I never thought it was very funny. One night in particular, I had a hard time producing the sample, and I got agitated. Fortunately for me, the class that night was particularly good, and I soon forgot about the minor problem that I had turned into a major problem.

The third phase of the program is really about the deeper meaning of faith, Bible study, and getting ourselves prepared for spiritual battle. One night, while studying in the book of James (one of my favorites), we started talking about how we must continue to pass the tests that we encounter on a daily basis. This lesson intensely moved me, and I felt the strong and purposeful presence of the Holy Spirit in the room. My confidence was growing as my faith was growing.

Testing Your Faith

When you are in a rehab program; drug and alcohol testing is the norm,
It's done for your protection to ensure your keeping safe and out of the storm;

Of recurring addiction; and regardless of your life-altering issue or drug of choice,
It's critical that you try and uncover the root cause and open your ears to hear the voice;

Of God; as you surrender, let your guard down and finally let Him in,
If you do this; the rehab process takes on new meaning, and you finally begin;

To understand what went wrong, what to do now, and where to turn,
In your time of need; with a new and reliable strength to discern;

Why God placed you in this specific rehab facility; and it all starts to unfold,
You were always meant to be here; to recover, so YOUR story can be told.

So others can learn from you when their lives become challenged and tested,
Because no one escape trials; the pain actually becomes unbearable if you are not vested;

In your belief system; the one true way; the way of Christ the King,
Your investment takes root, your heart opens, and that old familiar ring;

In your ear that speaks lies into your flesh; the resounding tune from down south,
Gets overpowered by truth, that you start to believe in your heart and speak through your mouth.

Your faith strengthens, and your tests seem lighter and much easier to overcome,
Because your Savior has provided you with purpose now; available to all; but only some,

Of us actually pass through the eye of the needle and understand that we can no longer afford,
To live life on our own, **it doesn't work**; the only way is redemption through The Lord.

> "Because you know that the **testing of your faith** produces perseverance."
> — James 1:3 (emphasis mine)

If there is one poem that has the deepest meaning for me, it is this one. So much so, I read this poem at my Fresh Start graduation in May 2014. I dedicate this poem to Marge and Mark Long, my guardian angels, through this time in my life. I entered this facility because of the two of you and was blessed that you could be there for my graduation. Love you guys.

Out of all the wonderful characters and co-authors of the Bible, Paul was certainly the one that attracted me the most. Being a writer myself and a self-professed "bad-guy," there was certainly some commonality there. I loved the way Paul wrote, spoke to people, and had such unrelenting faith. But it wasn't always that way for Paul. If you recall the Damascus Road experience, prior to that, Paul was living in sin and persecuting God's people. His ego was huge, and he lived his life on his terms, justifying what he was doing through the old laws, which were out of favor and wholly fulfilled through Jesus Christ. My *"spin"* on the Damascus Road experience has incredibly special meaning for me, as my life was truly transformed, and I was able to **start fresh** at this special place on the LAKE.

"Meanwhile, Saul was still breathing out murderous threats against the Lord's disciples. He went to the high priest and asked him for letters to the synagogues in Damascus, so that if he found any there who belonged to the Way, whether men or women, he might take them as prisoners to Jerusalem. As he neared Damascus on his journey, suddenly a light from heaven flashed around him. He fell to the ground and heard a voice say to him, 'Saul, Saul, why do you persecute me?' 'Who are you, Lord?' Saul asked. 'I am Jesus, whom you are persecuting,' he replied. 'Now get up and go into the city, and you will be told what you must do…' [Days later,] Placing his hands on Saul, [Ananias] said, 'Brother Saul, the Lord—Jesus, who appeared to you on the road as you were coming here—has sent me so that you may see again and be filled with the Holy Spirit.' Immediately, something like scales fell from Saul's eyes, and he could see again. He got up and was baptized, and after taking some food, he regained his strength."

— Acts 9:1-6, 17b-19

Lake Damascus

Paul was locked in chains, living in sin; driven to succeed and thinking he was on the right track,
Killing and persecuting God's people: an unthinkable crime; but then he was struck with an attack;

From our God in Heaven; an unusual choice for a messenger; one might think,
But that would be assumptive; because with our Lord and Savior there is always a link;

Between what we think we should be doing and what God really wants us to do,
Our purpose while we're here; our assignment; yes; that includes **me and you**;

We've traveled **our own** roads too long, and sometimes we invent lives that are fake,
Until we are confronted by a crystal clear and stark truth; either on a dusty road or by a lake;

For me; the truth has hit me hard and set me free; by a beautiful lake protected by My Savior,
Lake Damascus I call it; because this is where my life changed; as well as my attitude and my behavior.

I've come home to God, and I'm now ready to take my rightful place,
In His beautiful Kingdom; all by the amazing power of His love and His Grace;

And just like Paul; I can now see clearly; and my life will never, ever be the same,
No more self-pity, self- absorption, and certainly no more guilt and shame,

I was blinded like Paul, but my handicap was **money**; until I lost it all,
But now I realize what I'm supposed to do; it's now very clear to me that my new CALL;

Is to serve God and share my testimony with as many struggling addicts that I can possibly get TO,
I'm free at last, but don't take my word for it; try it for yourself. Again, that means **YOU**.

The one who thinks he has it all figured out, but we all know that there is something missing.
There's a gaping hole that can't be filled by money, possessions; not even hugging and kissing;

From members of the opposite sex; sure that feels good, but it's not the most important love,
The love OF God and FOR God is the most powerful force, and it comes from above.

And just like Paul; God will offer you opportunities to redeem and finally break the code,
Of a life unfulfilled, but through Christ, you still have time to find; your own **Damascus Road.**

Some of the greatest nights in recovery for me were the times when we had our Social Grams. What an amazing experience. It's a process where all 70 men in the program have an opportunity to share both a positive and a negative vote for one other brother; and then have an opportunity to speak into another man's life. It is a very tense setting, as you may imagine. It was so rewarding for me during these sessions to witness the life-changing moments in certain men's lives. I witnessed everything from brothers coming to Christ for the first time, to guys getting kicked out of the program, to flat-out life-changing processing scenes that blew me away through the power of the Holy Spirit. I thoroughly enjoyed this process; and learned so much about myself each time.

"We were therefore buried with him through baptism into death in order that, just as Christ was raised from the dead through the glory of the Father, we too may live a **new life**."
— Romans 6:4 (emphasis mine)

Social Gram

Seventy men lined up in a circle; anxiously awaiting another man's vote,
One affirmation; one caution; the Holy Spirit enters as each man starts to emote;

The votes get cast; first the positive, then the negative: one by one,
The event is intense; you can feel God's presence, and there is nowhere to run;

For shelter; as each man is exposed after careful thought, prayer, and preparation,
They get to look each other in the eye; the dialog starts flowing, and you can feel the sensation;

Of The Lord God Almighty as He speaks through these men on their journey through recovery,
And the enlightenment that they receive, if they are aware and present, can actually spark a discovery;

That could literally SAVE their life; at the very minimum, they will see spiritual change,
As they uncover their purpose; the true man God made them to be; it's time to rearrange;

Their hearts and their minds; they are growing under the protection and shelter of The Lord,
While they look deep inside, a light goes on; and with their shield and their sword;

They prepare for the battle; the one in the spiritual realm; when the enemy lurks,
These former addicts; renewed by the power of God; they used to feel like jerks;
But not anymore, their hearts are changing; their minds are opening; they begin to emerge,
With a stronger sense of who they are, no more false beliefs, they develop a strong urge;

To serve God and make their own unique and specific contribution,
Their eyes widen; their steps become lighter and swifter; no more retribution;

Equipped to share what they have learned through this well planned and meaningful exercise,
God smiles down on these reformed men, as they share their hearts; because to Him, it's definitely no surprise.

One of the true and lasting blessings of my time at Fresh Start was the humility I learned because of my genuine submission to the program. I decided early on that I was not going to get a vehicle for quite some time because the process of walking and taking the bus was truly rewarding. I used to walk miles and miles, especially on Saturdays. Some Saturdays, I would get up out of bed at 5 AM, and just start walking, leaving the property all day. I walked so much, I lost quite a bit of weight and even started to feel stronger.

In fact, if I were to change anything about that year, I would have waited even longer to buy a car. However, the lure to get back and visit my children on Saturdays was stronger. So, I gave in and purchased a vehicle in my 7th month in the program. Nevertheless, I will forever remember the specialness of those times of walking, listening to worship music, and communing with The Lord.

Walking the Walk

I get out of bed on Saturday morning, put on my clothes, and I just start to walk.
Each week I walk further, listening to music, worshiping The Lord; sometimes we talk;

About my journey, my children, my recovery, and I listen, and I wait,
For His signs, His word, especially now; that I am confident that my fate;

Is sealed, when it's over, I will face God and be in Heaven,
And while I walk today my steps seem lighter; and my engine is revvin';

I am feeling stronger and surer of myself; finally free from self-doubt,
My life is real now, empowered by my God, I know I can now survive without;

Worldly possessions, keeping up with the Jones', and having to perform for all to see,
Because there's only One I need to impress, My King; it's now much easier for me.

And it will be for you as well if you start walking this way, your life can truly change,
By the Power of God's Grace, it's closer than you think, easier to arrange;

Your priorities; your calling; not always thinking of yourself first,
You walk towards others in need, and you discover a new and undeniable thirst;

That can only be quenched by learning more about His word and His might,
And while you're walking, you start talking and sharing His message of Wisdom and light;

With people in your life; friends both new and old,
Your testimony shines a light on their feet, and God's plan starts to unfold.

You are now part of the solution; it's the only way to walk; do you see now?

This changes everything; others you encounter start walking with Him, and all you can say is "WOW."

> "When Jesus spoke again to the people, he said, 'I am the light of the world.
> Whoever follows me will never **walk** in darkness but will have the light of life.'"
> — John 8:12 (emphasis mine)

When I arrived at Fresh Start, one of the first things I needed to do was find a job. I made a list of about eight people I knew in the area, and the first phone call I made turned out to be the exact blessing I needed. I was able to land a job with some former colleagues, and my career was back on track in short order. Soon after I started, one of my business colleagues invited me to a Bible study called Man in the Mirror that met every Friday at 7 AM. Each week, I was able to share life with an incredible group of Christian men, and the lessons we learned from the leader of this group were invaluable to me on my path to recovery.

I dedicate this poem to my Christian brother, Thom Hollingsworth, who not only led me to this Bible Study, but he walked with me at work for the entire year. Love you, T.

Mirror Image

Each Friday morning in recovery, I attended a Christian men's group,
A blessing from a friend; an opportunity to learn more about My Savior and to recoup;

A chance to fellowship with other men of God; each with their own unique point of view,
While we unpack a message from an anointed spiritual leader; each week a new clue;

On how we can advance the Kingdom of God; as we acquire some new and useful tools,
To add to our man-belt; as we prepare for battle in a world filled with fools.

A world where most men really never get in the game; to them it's just a scrimmage,
Not an authentic game, the game that can only be played if we live in the Mirror Image;

Of God our Father; the One and only true King,
Who delivers us from evil; He offers new life for those of us who are willing to sing;

His praise and follow His purpose for our lives; now we just want to learn, to love, and to give,
Ourselves to God and to others, and this Bible study reminds me each week how a Christian man is supposed to live.

> "Do not merely listen to the word, and so deceive yourselves. Do what it says. Anyone who listens to the word but does not do what it says is like someone who looks at his face in a mirror and, after looking at himself, goes away and immediately forgets what he looks like."
> — James 1:22-24

As I mentioned, in Phase III of the program, we are challenged to dive deeper into the spiritual meaning of the lessons we are learning through recovery. It's a beautiful time, and for those who were taking the program really seriously, Phase III was an incredible time for growth. However, the lingering effects from the inner healing phase were ever-present; and for many men, these old feelings would rise up and haunt us while we were trying to ingest deep-rooted lessons. One day in particular, I was struck with a serious attack from the enemy. I was reeling with worry and anxious thoughts about my past and about the future. There was *"NO WAY"* that I could make up for my past mistakes, and I was on my way to depression. When I went into the Chapel to pray, I was overcome with emotion. God was waiting for me there. He reminded me that I was a new creation in Him and that I can't pour new wine into old wineskins.

> "I have given you authority to trample on snakes and scorpions and to overcome all the power of the **enemy**; nothing will harm you."
> — Luke 10:19 (emphasis mine)

Enemy Attack

When you are living in sin; life can sometimes seem fine,
Especially when you're wrapped up in Ego; it's often hard to see the line;

That you crossed in the spirit realm; because the world accepts this as the norm,
Your days go by, and the sin continues, but eventfully you face a storm.

One that you can't handle by yourself; so you get on your knees and pray,
To a God you don't know, and you cry out to Him, not knowing what to say.

And if you don't get a rapid response; you question and wonder why,
God is not listening; where is He? You feel empty inside as you try.

So you head back to where you came; the only way that you know,
But it's still not right; you're back in the darkness, again reaping what you sow.

Until you hit bottom again; and you finally realize,
That God is still waiting; it's YOU that needs to stand and rise;

To the occasion once and for all; and submit to His plan for your life,
And as soon as you do, the pain subsides, as well as the strife.

You come home to God just like the prodigal son;
Your heart transforms; your spirit comes alive: it's actually fun;

To live in God's will, and in His favor and His grace,
But now that you are a Christian, there are NEW trials you must face.

The enemy is angry; he had lost a companion; you're not the same man,
And he WILL attack with a new fervor; he will disguise his tricks any way he can.

You can be sure He will hit you where it hurts the most,
Places where you have fallen short before, just so he can boast.

When you fall again; because that is what most of us do,
But not this time; it's time for freedom, and new tools for you.

A new spiritual code that the enemy can't crack,
Regardless of how crafty and clever the attack;

Comes in and hits you when you least expect it,
But God is stronger than the devil, and you are now spiritually fit;

To handle anything he throws at you: no matter what it might be,
You're well on your way to living your purpose; you are finally set free.

On New Year's Eve, Fresh Start has a ceremony at midnight where we take communion and celebrate our relationship with each other and with Jesus Christ. Although I was sad to be away from my children, it was a special evening, and we were allowed to have our phones to connect with family. Pastor Joe asked us to decide on a word that would keep us focused on our walk with The Lord and our recovery for the upcoming year. My word for the year was **humility**.

"But when you ask, you must **believe** and not doubt, because the one who doubts is like a wave of the sea, blown and tossed by the wind."
— James 1:6 (emphasis mine)

It Is Finished

It occurred to me this morning that I've written something each New Year,
At least for the last several, but this piece is quite different; my vision is more clear.

My new lens is focused on the Creator of the Universe, the one and only; Jesus Christ.
And 2014 feels more promising than ever; I am free, no longer clamped in a vice.

Feeling worried and anxious as the virtual pliers grabbed and squeezed me so tight.
I used to write to release this grip, and it sometimes worked; that is until just a slight;

Shift in the wind, a trial, a tribulation; or another unwanted circumstance.
Entered my life, aligned with the enemy of this world, and I fell back into my trance;

Misery, an old friend, a comfort zone if you will, that held me in bondage to my pain.
The guilt from my past mistakes would reemerge and remind me again;

That I was really not a good person; how could I be when I behaved the way I did?
And the enemy's pursuit would intensify; because he knows that we struggle opening the lid.

The container of shame and suffering that can figuratively keep us frozen,
Until we wake up, look up, and realize we have an option; we are ALL God's chosen;

People; and the devil becomes devoid of power when we surrender and put our trust in God,
We know this is true; since it feels strange, a bit odd.

Uncomfortable even to really believe in things unseen and that we can truly be saved.
We've done so many bad things; some of us for years; can we really climb out of the cave?

Sure, we can; if our faith is strong, just like Jesus did when He escaped the tomb.
And after that day; He knew we could ALL be saved; as He knitted us in our mother's womb;

He also knew that we would have struggles; which is why He gave us all free will.
We are born sinners, in need of a Savior; but Jesus already paid the bill;

When He hung on a Cross for us, so, as we ponder what we will do in 2014.
Let us remember what He did that day; **it is finished**; we are all washed clean!!!

During Phase III, many men hit a roadblock, and it becomes difficult to ingest the daily message. You see, we are addicts, and addicts always think they have it figured out before they really have. This is a critical time in the program, and many guys leave during this phase. They believe they have "arrived" and are ready to face the world again. Unfortunately, there is a specific reason that the program is designed for an entire year. There are still things that need to be discovered. Now is the time where we need to start doing "our part" in what I call the "Division of Labor." How do we take our journey to the next level?

"Finally, be strong in the Lord and in his mighty power. Put on the full armor of God, so that you can take your stand against the devil's schemes. For our struggle is not against flesh and blood, but against the rulers, against the authorities, against the powers of this dark world and against the spiritual forces of evil in the heavenly realms. Therefore put on the full armor of God, so that when the day of evil comes, you may be able to stand your ground, and after you have done everything, to stand. Stand firm then, with the belt of truth buckled around your waist, with the breastplate of righteousness in place, and with your feet fitted with the readiness that comes from the gospel of peace. In addition to all this, take up the shield of faith, with which you can extinguish all the flaming arrows of the evil one. Take the helmet of salvation and the sword of the Spirit, which is the word of God. And pray in the Spirit on all occasions with all kinds of prayers and requests. With this in mind, be alert and always keep on praying for all the Lord's people. Pray also for me, that whenever I speak, words may be given me so that I will fearlessly make known the mystery of the gospel, for which I am an ambassador in chains. Pray that I may declare it fearlessly, as I should."
— Ephesians 6:10-20

What's Next?

OK, so now you are finally on your spiritual journey; now what?
Do your troubles disappear? Or is it that you're now able to find a slot;

A place to go where you can meet God and grab hold of His mercy and guidance?
A new discernment to sift through the rubbish of this world; to finally take a stance;

But you soon find out that the enemy is more powerful than ever,
You are not part of his team anymore; but he is still very, very clever;

Enough to know exactly where your weaknesses and pain points are hidden,
And he now works extra hard to get you back into sin; to taste the forbidden;

Fruit that is offered by this sneaky serpent; but we know that we must continue to fight,
That much harder now, it's time to dig in to reach a NEW LEVEL of wisdom and light;

The next level in our walk with God; we must keep our feet moving,
There are new hills to climb; we must stay focused and keep proving;

To ourselves and to our King that we are strong enough and deserving,
Of His almighty power and grace; it's our turn to start preserving;

The Kingdom of God; now we know we can out-duel the guy down south.
Because living a righteous life gives us supernatural power; and directly from our mouth;

We will speak truth and light; our hearts have changed; we are no longer perplexed,
We keep charging forward and now have answers to the question: WHAT'S NEXT?

The answer is simple; we keep pressing in to grow our relationship with The Lord,
Now perfectly equipped with strong armor; including a helmet, a shield, and a sword.

As the New Year began, I started feeling good about the direction of my life. How could I be so happy still living in a 70-man facility and away from my children? Finally, I started to feel like a real man, and I felt a new conviction about who I was becoming. Amen.

"Jesus replied, 'Very truly I tell you, no one can see the **kingdom of God** unless they are born again.'"
— John 3:3 (emphasis mine)

Stand or Fall - The Choice Is Yours

They say if you don't stand for something, you will fall for anything; could this really be true?
I think it is; I've tried the ways of the world where I was the one in charge; but I was still sad, lonely, and blue;

A feeling of security eluded me, and even though I had some as-semblance of worldly success,
I felt empty inside, insecure, putting up a false front, my life a complete mess.

I told others that I was open to all ideas, and there were many ways to get to your goal,
But now I realize that only ONE WAY is right: and that the enemy just flat out stole;

30 years of my life; how long will you linger here; and sit back and wait?
For the TRUTH to set you free. You see; complacency is attached to fate;

And when you don't stand on firm and solid ground and seek God's path,
You allow the evil one room to enter your spirit, and at some point and time; you WILL feel his wrath;

Which includes his plans for your life; a selfish path that has you believing that you can do this alone,
But when it's all said and done, will the devil be there in the end to help you atone?

For your sins, your self-centered ways, allowing in all of these ideas about the wrong ways to live,
That path leads to hurt, pain, and suffering; especially to the ones you wish to give;

Your blessings to and leave your legacy for; YES; your family and your children,
The beautiful people who really matter in your life; not the false illusion;

That the world creates that you must have this, live there; gather possessions and toys,
We all know that those things are fleeting; and that they are not meant for men; only boys;

And until you start standing for God, who waits to offer you His love, forgiveness and grace,
Your life will be unfulfilled, just like mine was, but now I am at home; and quite sure of my place;

In The Kingdom of God, my eternity is certain, sealed and secured,
And if I keep leaning in towards Him, my family will be safe, and we will no longer be lured;

By the pitfalls and evils of this world, it really feels great to live this way,
YOU can have it as well; if you just come home to God, let your heart change, and seize this day.

In the Phase II section, I wrote about the Social Gram and how amazed I was with this process. These were extraordinary times for me as I learned so much about myself through others. One Social Gram, in particular, stood out among the rest. It was one where I was "cautioned" by three different men—all with the same reasoning. It seemed as though my EGO, always my biggest problem, was still there, lingering in the background. These men picked up on it and had the courage to caution me during the event. The staff always asked us to examine what God was trying to tell us during this exercise. For me, it was crystal clear; *Humility* was still my snare.

"When pride comes, then comes disgrace, but with **humility** comes wisdom."
— Proverbs 11:2 (emphasis mine)

Humility's Snare

For many years I lived by my own accord; my own set ideas and of beliefs,
Life went by so quickly; it seemed a little strange to me; almost like a thief;

Was hiding in the shadows; just waiting to attack and bring me down,
But I ignored it and pushed away the feelings; never wanting to wear a frown.

The old me wanted to be known as someone who seemingly had it all,
A good life, a career, a family; those things were real; but I always feared a fall;

My EGO was so large I was able to mask the fear; thinking; "I" can do this; "I" know-how,
And the thought of being HUMBLE never really crossed my mind; I just wouldn't allow,

The guilt and shame I was feeling to seep into my pores; I was too busy with work and too focused on the cash,
Side-stepping the mines in the field, for a while anyway, but then came the crash.

You know; the moment in time where your wrongful behaviors rear their ugly heads,
And one day you wake up with nothing; you're broken, your tires have no treads;

The wheels of life start falling off; slipping and sliding all over the road,
Your lack of humility has caught you; again; and now your once heavy load,

Gets heavier; how could this happen to me; over and over again?
But you fall to your knees this time and pray; because with God you know still can,

Break these chains of self-righteousness; they were never really yours; you just wore them well,
And even now while you are getting better; they hang around; and someone rings the bell;

A reminder that Humility is still your Snare; it's your thing; it's still fresh,
But this time, it's not the dude down south; like Paul; it's the Thorn in Your Flesh.

And it will remain there so you can always identify from whence you came,
You keep pressing into to The Lord; He guides you and reminds you that you are NOT the same;

Man as you were before; you've changed; your wings have been untied; it's your time to fly,
You're learning to be humble, a new tool for your belt that will help you enter the Kingdom, in the beautiful blue sky.

Entering Phase IV of the program can be quite challenging. At this point, you are ready to go and get back to real life. However, there are still many items to uncover. For me, Phase IV was one of the most rewarding phases of my entire time at Fresh Start. It did not happen all at once; the early part of Phase IV was extremely hard for me. I was distracted, ready to move on.

"The thief comes only to **steal** and kill and destroy; I have come that they may have life and have it to the full."
— John 10:10 (emphasis mine)

Distracted Spirit

Distractions and interruptions in our spirit are inevitable and certainly something we have to face,
But when our momentum is halted by an outside influence, we recoil and quite often are struck with a case;

Of "I know best" or "it's this person's fault," we usually react quickly and shift the blame,
We avoid the mirror, pass judgment; and in most cases, we refuse to claim;

Any responsibility for our part of the equation or what God may be trying to show us through these trials,
After all, we always know best, right? It's the other people involved that are wrong and in denial.

But after we realize that these folks are just human, and they make mistakes just like you and me,
We come to grips with the truth and reality, and through the eyes of Christ, we learn to see;

This adversity that haunts our spirit for exactly what it is; a test designed for us to learn more,
About ourselves, about others; we see that now, and from deep in our core;

We uncover the fact that God allows us all free will to make our own decisions and choices;
And we learn to deal with situations better; we press in deeper to hear the crystal-clear voices;

Of the Father, the Son, and the Holy Spirit; our eyes open wide; it's now understood,
And life starts making sense again; objections become easier to overcome, and life is good.

And our Spirit that has been distracted comes alive again; we now feel whole,
And the peace that surpasses all understanding covers us completely and re-enters our soul.

Towards the end of my time at the Friday morning Bible study, there was a lesson on "abiding" in Christ. This lesson so moved me. Just the thought of "resting" in Him and having Him lead my life was so invigorating. For once in my life, I didn't have to be in charge. Jesus is in charge now. What a cool concept.

Decide to Abide and Reside

Our peace; or lack thereof; is the result of series of thoughts; which turn into decisions,
Choices that determine which type of life we will live; and quite often those purposeful revisions,

That we make on our journey are a byproduct of many things, but mostly how well we choose,
Which paths we will take, what we ultimately believe, even whether we win, or we lose.

It is truly up to each and every one of us to decide who and what we will be,
Who we will follow; where we will end up; and what type of legacy;

We will leave behind when we are done and have completed our earthly mission,
That's right; our assignment while we are here; and if it includes a complete submission;

To God's will for our lives; this unfolds for us as soon as we actually decide,
To put our trust in Him; stop living for ourselves; only then can we be free and finally reside;

In the peace and joy that accompanies a true relationship with the One who lingers above,
A partnership for all of our days; if only we will decide to abide and reside in His LOVE.

> "Remain in me, as I also remain in you. No branch can bear fruit by itself;
> it must remain in the vine. Neither can you bear fruit unless you remain in me."
> — John 15:4

During Phase IV, I started to reconnect with some people in my life in preparation for when I came out of rehab. One if the things I realized from talking with several people is that *"happiness"* and *"joy"* seem to be elusive in many cases. I have experienced a great deal of depression in my life, but the concept of "joy" is something I finally GET.

"Consider it pure **joy,** my brothers and sisters, whenever you face trials of many kinds."
— James 1:2 (emphasis mine)

Joy's Journey

Why does it seem so hard at times to hold on to the simple pleasantries in life,
We are faced with so many challenges; pain, disappointment, and certainly our fair share of strife.

Trials and tribulations that we face; it seems like we have so many worries and demands,
The elusiveness of JOY quite often feels like trying to hold water in your hands.

You can feel it, taste and drink it, it cleanses you; but it quickly goes away,
And once it's gone you don't think about it again until you are troubled, and much to your dismay,

Trying to hold on to this JOY can be an arduous and monumental task,
The pressures of life; financial, relational, and others that steer you back behind the mask,

That you wear to hide the pain; thinking that happiness is just not for you,
It's for the other people; they go on their merry way; you wonder why; and you again start to stew,

Over the trials in your life; what can they possibly have that I don't possess?
Why is my life so hard; people keep letting me down; why do I have so much stress?

Then one day, you awake, and something magical appears in your life and it lands on your doorstep,
Another glimpse of JOY enters your space, and you try your best this time to really accept,

This new and surprising blessing; perhaps finally it's my turn to enjoy,
My life again; your memory gets jogged regarding what this feels like, and you think; "Oh boy…"

"This feels really good; amazing; if I could just hold onto this wonderful feeling,
Could my life truly be better; is it actually possible to stop hurting and to stop reeling?

Back into the feelings of pain and sorrow that have haunted me for so long,
Is there some adhesive that can keep me here; can I start to sing a new song?"

As I prepared to exit my one-year commitment and enter my new life, thoughts of purpose and meaning covered me day and night. I was ready and now able to go out and actually LIVE my life's purpose. I was very excited, and my writing was starting to feel very authentic and intentional.

> "But I have raised you up for this very **purpose,** that I might show you my power and that my name might be proclaimed in all the earth."
> — Exodus 9:16 (emphasis mine)

Meaningful Lives

Quite often, I find myself in interesting and thought-provoking conversations,
About the meaning of life, how we each fit in the puzzle; and on many occasions;

The dialog elevates from a secular conversation to one of a more spiritual nature,
Does God really make us for a specific purpose? How can we be sure?

When we really sit back, and we start to think about our assignment on this earth,
We often get confused about our place, our job, our situation; and even our own self-worth.

We question the choices we make and wonder how we ended up in this barren and lonely place,
Our lives seem unfulfilled; scattered; are we living our lives, or just caught in the rat race?

Are we taking advantage of and utilizing our unique God-given talents and skills?
Do we see the fruits of the spirit when we look in the mirror, or are we still attached to the cheap thrills;

That we fall into when we let the enemy creeps into our days; blocking our spiritual assignment,
It clouds our judgment; until we stop; and remember that our God sacrificed everything the very moment He sent;

His only Son to this earth to live as a man and die for our sins, surely that act in itself should be enough,

For us to clear our minds and identify our one true purpose from all of this great stuff;

Our Heavenly Father bestowed on each and every one of us; talents meant to use,
To advance His Kingdom by setting an example for others; we have NO excuse;

We must walk out this righteous path, love our God and love one another,
The two basic Christian rules; if we are honest; we typically don't take the time to discover;

What we are really doing here on earth; what is our mission?
We are to use our talents to pour into others and to abide by the Great Commission;

To first become disciples and then go out and make more; YES; that is it,
We can finally stop striving for things we know we can't possibly reach; now we know that we fit;

Within the true purpose for our lives: a very poignant and simple concept; isn't it time for us to pull the lever?
If we do; our days on this earth will have true meaning; others will see our fruit; want what we have, and we will certainly; live forever.

Just before our class was set to graduate, we all went out bowling. Now, keep in mind, this was the FIRST time that we could go out of the facility in the evening the entire year. Yes, you read that correctly. The program is extremely strict and for valid reasons. This particular night was incredibly special, and I was part of the largest Phase IV class ever assembled at Fresh Start. There were ten guys in my graduating class, and sixteen in the Phase IV class overall. I will forever remember that particular evening.

"As iron sharpens iron, so one person sharpens another."
— Proverbs 27:17

Sharing Lights

According to the odds; the relapse rate for recovering addicts is close to eighty percent,
And if you are in a place covered by God's grace, the chances are better; but only if you represent;

Yourself in a manner conducive to following the light on the path that shines from above,
A path that includes surrender, focus, prayer, discipline, and an extra special helping of LOVE;

To love ourselves as God loves us, and to love ALL others in the very same manner,
The foundation of Christian faith, and regardless of the plight; we can ALL live under the banner;

Of Heaven; if we just have faith and believe that God will guide us and show us the right way to live,
We can beat these odds and break this cycle; we can repent, change our hearts and even learn to forgive;

Those people who we feel have contributed to our downfall; we would often deflect and place blame,
But when we look deep in the mirror, we finally take responsibility; these were **our** decisions; **our** shame;

We have learned how to deal with this pain through our recovery and the course of the last year,
This unique band of brothers, the largest **phase four** class ever, we no longer have to live in fear.

We have grown in Christ together; and my sense is that we will always have a special bond,
Sharing this journey has been amazing, even for this old guy; I feel proud and blessed beyond,

Measure; and I know that there is one thing that is an absolute guaranty for each of us as we depart,
We will no doubt struggle; the enemy will attack at a fierce pace and strategically place the dart,

In the bull's-eye of our weak points and our left-over snares; but there is also another sure thing,
We will ALL be there for one another, to help fight the demons, and with just one ring;

From one brother to another, we can ask for help; we've learned that we can't do this thing alone,
We need God, a body of special people; and this year at Fresh Start the new seeds were sown;

To be able to rely on God and each other in our time of need; when we face trials, and feel the light fading,
We must remember that we have **each other**; each willing to SHARE THEIR LIGHT; never again alone; never again evading;

Our troubles and turning back to our addictions; because our Lord and Savior now captains our ship,
And I am confident that this group of special men will find **success through faith**; and never, ever, again…slip!

In 2010, during the middle of my first attempt at recovery, I participated in a three-day deep cleansing spiritual class specifically designed to get your head clear and get your life back on track. It was a detailed evaluation, sharing, coaching, and spiritual healing— guided by a special person trained to help people refocus their lives. During one class, we were asked to write a poem from the future version of who we would become in ten years. I had never written a poem before in my life. So, I wasn't exactly sure what I would write. I took a deep breath, and in about two minutes, I wrote this poem. My faith was suspect, and I wasn't close to God while I wrote it. Looking back now, He was guiding me the entire time—always loving me, always watching over me, waiting for me to come home to Him. Waiting for me to befriend the mirror.

Thank you, Jesus.

I Am

Written by the future version of Tony Caico (2020)

I am a wise and humble soul.
Peaceful, I am.
Patient, I am.
It took me a while, but that's OK.
Grateful, I am.
Fulfilled, I am.
I started down my path, but it was cluttered.
Persistent, I was.
Focused, I was.
The path led to the purpose.
Confident, I became.
Authentic, I became.
My journey continues; what a great feeling.
Contemplative, I am.
Present, I am.
The mirror and I are finally friends.

> "See, I am doing a new thing! Now it springs up; do you not perceive it?
> I am making a way in the wilderness and streams in the wasteland."
> — Isaiah 43:19

In conclusion, to shine the light where it belongs and give glory to my King, I will add one more defining piece to my restoration journey. The poem "I Am" shines the light on me. As if, somehow, I could take credit for what happened to me at that beautiful place by the lake. I cannot. All of the glory goes to My Lord and Savior. You see, the title of my previous poem is "I Am," and those two words can only represent one person: Jesus Christ. Therefore, I will conclude with a piece I penned from the now-saved version of this grateful, redeemed author. I realize that this journey is a lifelong process, and someone incredibly special to me encouraged me to add this piece to the end of this book. Ultimately, the light should shine the brightest from its Source.

Just because we become Christians, life does not automatically get better. On this side of Heaven, strife and difficulties fill our lives— the book of John confirms this when Jesus says, "I have told you these things, so that in me you may have peace. In this world you will have trouble. But take heart! I have overcome the world" (16:33).

This reality hit me hard recently, and it suddenly dawned upon me: My true, authentic identity now comes from a new source—no longer myself—but from My Lord, Jesus.

I Am Because He Is

I still sin, which makes me a sinner. I still lie, even little white lies, which makes me a liar.

I still swear, I still take shortcuts, I still boast, I am still selfish, and all of that makes me a flawed human in need of a Savior.

The good news is that my Savior saved me, my Lord loves me, my God forgives me, my Holy Spirit guides me, my King protects me, my Friend never leaves me, and my Jesus died for me and now lives in me.

He is, well...EVERYTHING.

So, I am good.

> "Blessed is the one who perseveres under trial because, having stood the test, that person will receive the crown of life that the Lord has promised to those who love him."
> — James 1:12

www.ingramcontent.com/pod-product-compliance
Lightning Source LLC
Chambersburg PA
CBHW061113070526
44583CB00027B/3275